This work Copyright © Katriona MacMillan. Reserved.

Katriona MacMillan reserves all rights to be identified as the moral author of this work. All thoughts, ideas, and events expressed were her own fault. This book or any portion thereof may not be reproduced (either digitally, metaphysically, figuratively, or diabolically) in any way, without the express permission of the author. You may quote from it, but you will probably want to paraphrase.

First Printing 2020.

Cover Art © Katriona MacMillan, 2020.

Queries to the author may be addressed if you can find her.

The Online Content Writer's Handbook

By Katriona MacMillan

Introduction
For those that have Truly Thought This Through.

If you are anything like me, you are probably either a Millennial or a Gen Z writer – maybe younger.

You are likely a writer by trade – although more likely you don't think you are a professional yet... even if you have been writing every day for the last few years. We are like that. As a breed of human being we have little confidence and huge amounts of stubbornness. It's an apt replacement when it comes to hard work.

Anyway, nobody came here to listen to my opinions on the emotional make-up of a writer – we are here to learn how to write **online content**. The reason why I started banging on about writers is because, historically speaking, we have always been poor.

Money doesn't come in unless you work for one of the big publishing houses. You might have a handful of EBooks that do OK, but that aren't making you enough to live on. You might even be published in ten different places and still not be making an income... if this sounds familiar then you have come to the right place. In addition, we should probably network cause that's basically my life story.

No tricks, no gimmicks, no promises that you will make a million in a fortnight... Just this: if you write online content as part of the gig economy you can make enough to live on, just by writing. I know because I've been doing it for a while now. If you are good enough you can earn a decent rate, if you are gifted you can earn as much as you like.

You're self-employed, you work from home (or wherever in the world you happen to be) and all you really need is a laptop and an internet connection. Yes, you do need to write pages about gym flooring or the sustainability of Tallaly rubber... but you learn a lot. Do it enough and you become a sort of walking dictionary of useless information. People will start rolling you out at parties to spout off facts. You become *that* person... someone only describable by way of italics.

What Do I Know?

I have about 3 years of experience in the online content writing field. My daily word count is 3k – with a 2k absolute minimum if I get sick or something terrible happens in life. I have been writing every day for three or four years now - but writing fiction since I was 14. I was one of those angst-ridden teenagers who wrote bad poetry with swear words in it and called it "poetic license".

Many years later I handwrote my first novel while sitting in the bathroom of my halls of residence at uni. It was dissertation year. The bathroom was the only place in the building you could smoke without getting caught. Everyone else was complaining about reaching 10k words in their dissertation and I was worried about leaving the word count a hundred miles behind me in the dust. I wrote about the 'Braveheart' portrayal of Scotland by Hollywood. To this day it remains the worst thing I have ever written. I hope someone burned it.

My first book was decent. You can still buy it on Amazon. It starts a series of high fantasy magical weirdness with some dark humour and a good adventure or two thrown in...

Now that the shameless plug on my fiction (it's called *Edelweiss*) is out of the way - maybe I can tell you why I feel qualified to write *this* book[1].

Editing's a Bitch

It is. I've had to sort/fix/re-write/burn work by a hundred other content writers. I have had to re-research things that didn't make sense. I have been sent stuff where the link the writer used wasn't even to the client's website. Seriously. I've corrected bad translations, thrown awful English in the bin and completely started whole pieces again. All this while working for one of the many, many, *many* writing agencies that are springing up all over the place.

I'll talk more about writing agencies in a bit, I want to finish listing my awesome achievements first...

I got the best scriptwriting qualifications I could get at Uni. A few years before that I studied English Lit and Grammar at Glasgow University for two semesters (it was really posh, I felt like a fish climbing a tree). I learned a little Old English which was amazing. I studied a TEFL in my own time a couple of years back as a new string to my bow, too.

Three years after I made the commitment to myself to start writing all the time, I now have three different self-published books. People say self-published works don't count. The hundred odd hours I spent working on each one and the monthly pay I get from them begs to differ. It is my opinion that the future of literature lies in self-publishing. That being said I

---

[1] Edited to add that I have made the top ten freelancers on PPH list a few times now... just saying...

have signed a book contract with a third party too. I don't have a literary agent because I haven't felt the need for one yet. Nowadays, I think, we have to find the work on our own.

So... with a steady-but-low book income, five or six published short stories that other people were making money from, and the stubbornness that seems inherent to all writers: I decided to find a new way to make money writing.

I started to think about webpages and blogs. I realised that there are a billion websites out there and only a small minority of the population who can write like me. So who was writing their stuff for them? I could do that, make some money, and move up in the world. I was still working in Kitchens and had been since high school. I have nothing but respect for chefs and porters, but it wasn't what I wanted to do with my life. All the time I spent in kitchens I was coming home and writing.

For years it went on this way. I worked, came home and wrote, ate, slept, and repeated. I fell into the work rut. I churned out words like butter and forgot about my social life. By year six I noticed the content writing market was huge, joined a site and watched as nobody hired me. Like it or not I had no experience in a huge but evolving market. I took an offer working for the agency and wrote for peanuts until I had enough experience to get out of there.

Now you know a little about me, maybe you can trust me enough to learn from this guide. I understand that Google changes algorithms and all the rest – but content writing is content writing. If you can learn the techniques in the same way that there is a difference between writing a poem and writing an essay, then you should be able to apply those techniques to any changes that come along in the future.

Let's get stuck in, one imposter to another, and find out how we can make you churn out words, too.

Online Content Writing starts by being Unique

Straight up. If you want to copy and paste, then feel free to let the door hit you on the way out. This is for serious writers only. Writers need to physically write in order to earn their name. This also won't work for anyone who thinks they can create a list of phrases and cut them together when they need a new piece. Just forget it.

Is Online Writing for Me?

If you keep a blog of your own, then you already qualify. If you can spew out vast quantities of regurgitated information? This will make you a flaming fortune.

The best kind of writer to create online content are those that have absolutely no fear of ideas ever 'running out'. The types of writer who have heads full of stories they will never possibly get around to writing because there isn't enough time in a single lifetime. If you can say the same phrase three different ways in one paragraph, then you know you have the stuff that makes a great content writer. It's part ideas, part imagination, and part being able to re-word the same things over and over again for the purposes of remaining plagiarism free.

Let's be a bit clearer than that: you shouldn't repeat anything in a single article. If you are writing forty-two articles about cheeses, then you are going to need to learn to repeat the same information in 42 different ways – you get me?

So if you are thinking of taking up content writing then try a little test on yourself.

If you can re-write the following sentence 5 times in 5 different ways but keep the same meaning, then you might just be damned good at this...

"There is a vast difference between the luxury found in the hotels of Dubai, to that found in the opulence of the Riviera."

If you got on OK with that one then stick with it, content might just be your ticket to success.

Is there really Money to be Made?

Do you think I would be putting my time into this manuscript if there wasn't? The gig economy is on the rise. In Britain (where I am) the Office of National Statistics reported 90,000 new self-employed workers since last year. That's a 14% increase[2] - we are seeing the highest rates in history – and they are putting it down to gigging. The Guardian puts the number of Britons who make money from the gig economy (in 2019) at 4.7 million. Let that sink in.

Nearly 5 million other people are already making money from home. They're not all writers but I'd bet my imaginary millions that a good fifth of them are. Some on the side and some full time. That doesn't mean you are going to make a killing, but it is clear evidence of demand. One of the best tools you have at your disposal is that English is your first language. Everyone else

---

[2]https://www.ons.gov.uk/employmentandlabourmarket/peopleinwork/employmentandemployeetypes/articles/labourmarketeconomiccommentary/may2019

in the world that is building a website and doesn't speak English is therefore a potential client.

I mean you don't even need a degree anymore. The ability to string a sentence together and argue about why you are grammatically correct (even if you're not) is qualification enough. It's like English became politics and politics became a horror/comedy.

Anyway.

Should You Write for an Agency?

This is why there are states in America trying to limit how much work you can do per month, per client. Agencies rip writers off. It is what they are designed to do. Before we get to whether or not you should work for one, let's talk about how they work to swindle you.

An agency and an anthology work in similar ways. You are hired as a writer to write something for a meagre rate, or you are invited to submit a story for free.

In the case of the anthology, they will pick the best ten stories of the five hundred they were sent, send you a free copy, publish for a tenner a shot, then leave you with nothing for your trouble. You get the published writer credit though. Is it worth it? Maybe not. Without that published writer credit nobody will hire you though. It's your call.

Similarly with agencies, you will find there is one writer at the top. This person has a good reputation and makes $25 per article. They get the assignment, pass it on to their pool of writers, and one of us idiots writes it for five bucks or less. Again

– you might not want to take the work but without it you don't get a foot on the ladder.

So my advice to you is yes; write for an agency. Submit a few articles then demand better pay. If they don't give you it then move on. You will have your published online content/short story writer credit and you can now get better paid work. Take a spoonful of humility. Everyone has to start at the bottom, even Gods. Ask the late, great Terry Pratchett.

What About Competitions?

I came back to this section to add in a little about competitions. I recently encountered a Scottish charity who are supposedly in existence to support the Scottish Arts. They are charging new writers only (because professionals don't fall for this sh*t) £10 to submit a short story to their competition.

Now I have given stories to charity before. They approached me and asked me to help the cause and I did it. There is no way in an ice-cube-ridden-Hell I am paying someone ten quid so they can put together an anthology including my work. They keep the royalties and they get my tenner? What?

This from a charity meant to support the arts...

So the warning: If you need to pay to submit; don't submit. We can't encourage this type of rubbish and expect to make a real wage. Writing is a career. It's not a hobby or a competition. It's work... and anyone willing to take your money and have you work for free is asking too much. Would you expect an electrician to work for free because you are a charity? No. Well then.

But yeah, I'm totally over it.

Is Grammar Important?

Nobody cares in content. If you can spew out a thousand words an hour, then seriously: nobody cares. Many people will tell you your grammar is bad. Most of them won't have English as a first language. The thing is; if they can make you believe your writing is trash then they can pay you less. Fact. Don't fall for it (clearly, I did).

Other notes on grammar? Nobody cares… but nobody cares even less if you are consistent about your mistakes. Consistency is arguably more valuable than grammatical knowledge. If it is keeping you awake at night, then use a word-type program that includes a grammar check. Easy.

Bad grammar isn't a barrier to success in any other field, after all.

As a later edit: I recently started working with a client that DOES care about grammar. They are pretty easy to avoid though. For the most part, they want you to use website grammar. This involves obscure ideas like keeping your paragraphs to a two sentence maximum and retaining Flesch reading scores relevant for five year olds. Eww.

What about ideas?

Ideas are never overrated. If you write fiction, then fantastic. However you generate ideas for fiction is how you do it for content.

The clients that come to you have a set of keywords to hit so that they are found among their competitors. What you say in between those keywords is more-or-less up to you. The more imaginative you are, the better. Most of the time a client wants business-like, professional script. Once in a while you get one who lets you loose properly though. Those times you can be as daft as you like, as long as those keywords are hit and filled with unique content.

The more tangents you go on; the better. If you know loads of random facts? Excellent. All of it will help.

If you are stuck for ideas, then I suggest the "What If?" game. For example: I am on article 38 of 40 cheese-based descriptions. I already ran out of interesting ways to say "it's yellow" twenty articles ago. So I start to play What If? What if I was an alien and had never tasted cheese before? Can I describe the taste fully, so that even a lactose intolerant would drool?

What if the moon was made of cheese? Actually? What if it rained cheese? What if we were floating in a Universe of cheesy asteroids and they started to fall to earth? So then I start writing like I'm scared of cheese, like a cheese-phobic...

Another great way to turn something into content is to use a listicle. More on those later; but basically take the content subject matter and add a "The top ten best _____" on the front. Other attention-grabbing headlines include the likes of "Tops Tips for _____", "What the experts don't want you to know about ____" and other such click-bait nonsense.

Hopefully you get the idea.

How to Practice

You can put together a few good articles for yourself simply by copying and rewording. We call this "article spinning" in the business. While I am not normally a fan of rewording someone else's work I do recommend it as a way of training.

So go online, pick a five hundred word webpage at random, then re-write it in your own style. If you enjoy reading it back, then you could be on to something. If you find it excessively difficult then don't be surprised. You are forging new ways of thinking. Do this a few times and it will get much easier.

Now take what you have written and run it through a plagiarism checker. You can use Copyscape (which is widely accepted as industry standard) but it needs to be paid for. If you don't want to plough any money into this until you are earning, then use a different site. There are plenty of free ones out there to choose from.

I always recommend awareness of your surroundings as practice. How many hours a day do you spend online getting lost in trashy articles exactly like these? Notice them, remember what drew you in, and emulate that next time you sit down to write - but from a fresh perspective.

LSI Keywords

Latent Semantic Indexing Keywords. Yeah. It's the broken down way of saying people will want you to use synonyms and other words related to their topic. If you do that, they score higher in algorithms. Or something. Just put them in and don't ask. They do particularly well in subheadings (as do all keywords).

Other Considerations

What else to think about when writing online content? You should keep your keywords handy and make sure you hit them. The rest is pretty much structure based. I hope you have enjoyed my little summary so far – but let's get down to business. Online content is mostly about formatting and structure. It is when you have to churn out 3K a day that you need to start worrying about where the ideas will come from.

Formatting (Where it's At)

Changing any type of writer into an online content writer is largely dependent on their ability to format. If you have ever tried to design the layout of your own book, then you already know the struggle.

All articles have a certain few things that help them stand out in search engines. There are things that all pieces of online writing should have, then there are the things that only some need, and then there is the more specific stuff. Don't know what I mean? That's fine, don't give up yet.

Let's start with the things that all online articles are expected to have, without fail.

Things all Articles Need to Have

1 – Short Sentences
Apparently, the modern reader has less of an attention span than your average goldfish. I have had clients specifically request each sentence be less than 15 words. Generally speaking, they don't stay clients for long… It's a good guideline, nonetheless.

2 – Short Paragraphs
Keep your paragraphs to 5 lines maximum. This is that attention span thing again. Conversely, you should make them shorter the younger your reader.

3 – Some sort of List
Bullet points always go over well. Clients often ask for lists as it makes the algorithms pay attention. Most of the time they

don't care what the list is about as long as it relates to their content. It can be bullet points or numbers, again, nobody really minds. Legend has it, it's an algorithm thing.

There is also a school of thought that says people skim an article and only stop to read the bits that apply to them. When you skim, the first thing you notice is the lists or the bullet points. Try it for yourself next time and see what you notice first.

4 – References (and citations where possible)

Harvard referencing isn't always necessary, but you should insert a footnote or endnote wherever you feel your knowledge is likely to be questioned. It not only shows the client you did your homework; it also establishes them as an authority to their customers. Everyone wins. I am a great believer that the link has replaced the reference, but if you are writing something that *isn't* online content, the reference still stands.

5 – Links – Unless Specifically Otherwise Stated

Links can be tricky to get the hang of. Put at least three links into each article but none into webpages. For example, if I were writing a blog, I would link to all of my sources except competitors. If I were writing a home page for any firm I wouldn't link anywhere but would insert inspirations as endnotes for the client to review or remove as they see fit.

6 – Accurate, Unique, Up-To-Date Information

For goodness sake don't make stuff up, you will get caught. Your client is likely to be extremely well-versed in what they do, what they make, or what they sell. Just do some research before you write. It's easier in the long run and the next time a client from that industry reaches out to you, you will already have the experience. If you write something and a client doesn't want it? Feel free to keep it for someone else.

7 – More Words than Ordered
If someone orders a 500 word blog post you better give them 550 words, at least. Give them wiggle room. An extra paragraph that they can use if they don't like some of it. If you really hate a client, then give them 500 words on the nose. Ahem.

8 – Use all the Keywords
Use all the keywords around 3 times. A client will ask for more or less if they want it. Try to make one of those times in a heading. Headings are important since they usually carry more weight with search engines.

9 – Include Backlinks
Each blog post should link to another blog post, information page, home page or to the contact details of the client. Backlink up to (but no more than) three times. It is all about being natural. If the firms who run the search engines think you are not writing normally then they will drop you down the ratings. Some clients ask for between 3 and 5 times and that's pretty normal. I just prefer to err on the side of caution with this subject.

10 – Know your Content Types
You need to familiarise yourself with the different types of online content that there are out there. We are about to look at each in more detail but, broadly speaking, these are the subgroups:

- The Blog Post – used by firms to hit keywords, usually posted weekly.
- The Press Release – used by companies to announce new products or genuine company news.
- The News Article – sometimes clickbait, sometimes genuine journalism. Both types pay.

- The Online Copy – Webpages; home page, about us page, services pages, contact us pages – any type of page you read, you will be asked to write at some point.
- Product Descriptions – self-explanatory. If you see a product on Amazon and the description is well written, it was one of us.
- Reviews – dodgy area, but some people will ask you to write product reviews. Go to Amazon, look through comments, if the review is 500+ words – it was one of us.
- Miscellaneous – there are a myriad of other things. Short stories, letters of recommendation, CVs – all stuff that isn't really online content, but that you get asked to do pretty often. Use your own moral compass to negotiate the mire.

Try not to write anyone's research papers, exam papers, or high school essays for them. Nor anything you think is morally below the belt. You can make a lot of money writing for escort services and other morally ambiguous places. The choice is yours. There's a whole market for it and frankly, I'm surprised more writers aren't involved in that industry… I guess folks are too busy looking at the pictures to worry about the words.

Equipment

What do you need to get started? You need a laptop (doesn't even have to be fast) and a working internet connection. You also need some kind of typing program. Notebook isn't going to cut it so choose one with a spellcheck system. Grammar checking software is also good.

As I think I mentioned before you don't need much, and you can do it with just those three things. However, if you are writing a novel and doing bulk editing by yourself you can invest in something like Grammarly or Smart Edit. I prefer Smart Edit for novel and story writing but Grammarly for online content. It is good at measuring sentence length.

Again, Copyscape is the industry standard for checking against plagiarism but there are plenty of free versions out there. In addition, you don't need Microsoft Word, Open Office will do. Google Docs have a free document writing facility that has the best voice dictation I have found so far. There are loads of options for cheap alternatives.

You don't even need a printer to write online content. Nor do you need an English degree. All you need is the ability to show up and write every day. If you can handle that, it's pretty easy. Plus you learn a lot.

Carry a pen and paper on you at all times, which is easier for us girls than it is for those that don't have a handbag. I'm sure you will rock the man-bag if you need to commit. It's a work thing. You'll be fine.

Your portfolio is the most important tool you have. Since you are working online, you need it to be an online one. Never throw anything away and always, always, always save an online copy. I use One Drive. Others are just as good.

Oh and endless amounts of coffee. Virtually every writer I know needs it as a matter of life and death. It's creative juice. Don't fight the coffee.

Formatting 500 Word Blogs and Articles

This is the hardest bit. Once you get it right you are on your way to writing anything you like.

Set your page up as follows:

- 11/12pt script
- Calibri, Times New Roman or Courier. Arial is sometimes asked for but not as often as it used to be.
- Normal line spacing – unlike any other form of submission in the English language writing system; no extra spacing is needed.

As a bonus, you don't really need these settings they are just 'industry standard'. DO NOT hand anything back in Comic Sans, it will get deleted. Apart from that you are pretty safe.

So how do you shape a decent SEO blog/article/piece? Like so…

The Beginning

Main Heading – Also called H1, probably just because that is the formatting title, they want you to use from Word. Always use one H1, at the top and centre of the page just like you would expect.

To optimise it for clients make sure you use the top keywords. This is a general rule for all titles. It helps the search algorithms pick them up faster.

Meta Description – Follow a main title with a Meta. This is the one or two sentence description that comes below the title of a blog post or webpage when it appears in search listings. If you are writing web pages, it will describe the brand you are selling. If you are writing a blog, you don't really need this. I like to include them just because they are fun, catchy, and work like a subtitle.

After your H1 and your meta, introduce your piece. Again, two or three lines with a maximum of five. You can have one or two paragraphs here and it's acceptable. Even three works as long as they are less than 150 characters... yes, someone measured it, it wasn't me it was WordPress.

The Middle

The middle should start with your second heading. Use H2 in word as this is industry standard. Clients might ask for something else and that's fine. The heading should always contain as many keywords as you can naturally fit in.

Whatever the subject matter, use the H2 space to give the simplest explanation of what your title talks about as you can. Subsequent paragraphs and headings will go into detail. This ensures you always have something to write about.

If it is a 500 word piece, then one paragraph here is enough. Two is the very most you should write before moving on to the detail of answering the question, listing the products, or giving your guide. In a thousand word piece you have the full three paragraphs to get to your point here. This is where the format changes a little.

Two Different Endings

So far, our content looks like this:

Main Heading or H1

Bringing You Headlines Since 1994. We give you a bit of explanation as to what the subject is about. This first paragraph always contains the keywords that are in the heading. In this case it might be "Main Heading or H1 – what's your choice?". You get the idea.

You can also have a bit more here to invite them in using targeted phrases. I might say "read on to learn all about it", "Keep ahead of the trends by learning...", or something to that effect.

The Second Heading Goes Here

After which I give a more detailed explanation about what the choice really is. Why does anyone care whether we use H1 or Heading 1? If nobody cares, this is your opportunity to tell the reader why they should care about it. In fact, you have to suggest that their ignorance might be a problem for them in future.

Don't forget:
- Companies like bullet points
- Remember them in every article you do
- There don't need to be more than three
- But shoot for five.

What if someone were to ask you your opinion at a dinner party? What if you didn't have an opinion? What if you had to choose between Heading 1 and H1 right there and then? Nobody likes to be put on the spot... get your opinion now, before it's too late! In fact... we happen to know where you can buy them...

This is where we split off. If you are in a five hundred word piece you add in a bit about the company/product that you are selling. You can add in benefits, make it sound as good as you can and give as accurate a description as possible.

So when we get to the point above in a five hundred word article, we will probably use one more H2 (although the article might not need it) and then round up with a conclusion. Your conclusion will be an H3 and will usually point back towards the firm paying you to write.

If you can master that format for five hundred word articles you will soon be churning them out. You also get five hundred word listicles, which are a little different, but we will cover them shortly. Don't forget to always give your client more than the word count, so shoot for 550-600 words for each one.

Let's move on to turning that 500 words into a 1,000 word piece.

Writing 1,000 Word Content Pieces

Taking that 500-word article up to a thousand words isn't as hard as you think it is. It *feels* hard because you have double the words to write. Naturally, this takes double the time. On occasion you will sit for a while scratching your head, wondering how to fill the words.

It doesn't need to be this way. Let's go back to the last page and work from that first H2.

Title {H1}

Intro about how awesome paragraphs are when you really get to know them.

H2 or Heading 2 goes here

Then we have a paragraph that describes the basic elements of the topic. Say you are writing about why carrots make you see in the dark. You might mention here that it is an old wife's tale – at first glance... but is there something to this?

Then another paragraph explaining how old wives' tales usually have a speck of truth to them. You might give an example of this: like eating your crusts made your hair curly. Although that's not true; curly hair was seen as attractive back-in-the-day. If that's the case, then eating your crusts would have been a great way to make sure kids ate their meals.

H2 or another Heading 2

So now we have a second H2 – which is fine, you can have as many as you like. Remember to keep adding those keywords. We can put our bullet point list wherever we like except the intro or conclusion. Some people like to do a 'key takeaways' piece at the start, some like to use it to round up.

We want to keep running with H2 unless we come across a subtitle. Like the example given below. If you are a native English speaker there is a high chance you already know what the difference is, just by feel. If not? How the Hell did you get this far?

But seriously, if you're not a native speaker or if you want to know the grammatical rule for deciding between an H2 and an H3; it's this. H3 can always be divided up into sections of an H2. So: listing types of the same thing? That's a bunch of H3s under an H2 heading. See below for an example in action.

Why Humans Can't See in The Dark? {H2}

Why do we need to see in the dark anyway? What possible benefit to us is seeing in the dark? We have lights nowadays, and torches. Maybe we stopped evolving to need to see in the dark. If humans hadn't built torches – would we have evolved that way?

Let's look at these animals and see if they evolved that way... what about this vole? How do bats do it? If we fed carrots to bats would they suddenly stop being blind?

Let's look at what the science says...

The Science Behind Carrots {H2}

Another paragraph, this one discussing the scientific studies that back up your theory. As it turns out, there is a chemical compound in carrots that is actually great for the sight. This means that, even although the original phrase might have come from an old wives' tale – it just might be true!

We might look out a few more studies next. Here are some of the studies we have dug out, just for you:

- This is where you put your lists in.
- Firms like bullet points because it scores high in the rankings.
- It makes them seem like they know what they are talking about.

So as you can see; there are loads of studies about carrots. Let's go into some of them in more detail.

H3 – Carrot study 1
Carrots taste great

H3 – Carrot study 2
Not everyone likes them

H3 – Carrot study 3
I think they're awesome

Overall, Carrot Scientists Agree on One Thing!

What is that one thing? I don't know when I set out to write the article, but I know that hooks in the titles draw in readers. I also know that I hit some of the keywords in the same title, so it works on two levels. If I wanted to be super-cool, I would add in an alliteration... assonance is the way forward...

When did I start making grammar jokes? No matter. At this stage we would repeat switching between H2 and H3 until the conclusion. In the conclusion don't mention anyone new. The rest of the rules are basic essay writing. I may do another book on that in the future so watch this space.

In the meantime, we are about to move on to the listicle. A few more thoughts on the thousand words though: keep linking and add in your references as endnotes. If you say something, make sure you can refer the reader to the place you got it from.

You only need a single H1 per article, make sure you use it to hit as many keywords as you can. Oh and use Spellcheck and any editing system you have. Open Office has a great one nowadays that will help you stay on track.

If you are writing 1000 word + articles, then first of all – look at you! Secondly, just keep switching between H2 and H3 unless you are doing new chapters or new pages. Avoid taking on huge articles straight away though. There is nothing worse than running out of things to say.

Writing a Listicle

It's a real word, I swear.

A listicle is all of the articles that you would consider to be clickbait, without being news. So anything that starts with a number, basically. Some examples are:

- The top 10 best shopping carts of 2020.
- The 7 greatest artists of the 19th century.
- 3 ways to build business through social media!
- Grow your online store in these five easy steps.

You get the idea.

How to Write Listicles?

The Listicle is the easiest type of article there is. You can fire through ten of these in a day once you get to a good word count. There are a few things to consider before we get to format though.

The main concern is how many points your client has and whether they will all fit into the word count. The most you will get away with inside of 1000 words is 20 – and that's at a huge push. I've only managed it once and I was so far over the word count it took as long to trim as it did to write.

Ideally, 7-10 points fits nicely into the thousand-word mark. I have stretched five to fit many times before, too. Nobody ever wants 15; but the next step up is usually 20. Unfortunately nobody told your clients this and they are going to ask you for twenty points in five hundred words.

It is your job and your duty to turn them away from these decisions. Commonly, they will argue that a ten-point article in 1K words gives you a hundred words per point. They forgot to include the introduction and the conclusion, as well as whatever else makes it look good. More and more clients want picture links to social media pages. It's fine it just takes time.

Other things to consider with listicles are what your clients are selling. As well as your usual backlinks to their site, you will also need links to their products. Say it is entitled "The Top 10 Garden Chairs of This Season" – the client will have one of two motivations. They will either be purveyors of garden furniture, or they sell stuff on Amazon through their site.

In this instance, taking your links from Amazon earns them cash if you sell it well enough. It's a common way to do business and, if you have your own blog, it's worth a shot. Anyway... this is a big part of the reason I always ask a client where their article will be used. It helps me to decided what links they want.

Another problem: sometimes clients don't know what type of links they want... and you need to make the call that makes them happy, before they know it's what they need. One-part writer, two-parts psychic.

Let's get on with the format... it's incredibly easy.

The Top 3 Reasons this is the Best Book Ever {or H1, I always centre H1, just FYI}

META: EVERYONE Should Buy My Book! Why? Read on To Find Out...

There are three main reasons why everyone in the world should be reading "The Online content Writer's Handbook". I am about to tell you all about these wonderful reasons – but first I want to make you feel good about yourself, so that you know I am warm and inviting.

You have lovely hair today. Now that's out of the way, let's get down to business. Why should you buy my book? I'm about to tell you!

Three Reasons to Buy My Book {H2 – but notice repetition of the title. The first H2 should always try to repeat as many keywords as possible. If a client hasn't given you specific keywords it is because they want, you to use the title as the keyword set}

There are three really fantastic reasons to buy my book. In fact, they're so amazing that you probably won't believe me!

1 – it's an Awesome Book! {H3}

Honestly! I love it and I never like anything I write. If I love it, it must be good... Fool proof.

2 – there may be Dragons in my Book! {H3}

There aren't – but I bet that made you think it was awesome!

3 – it was Written with Love!

Or at least lessening degrees of hostility, since I quit smoking in November.

Rounding Up {H2 – Optional. Some clients like to leave it hanging. I never leave it hanging. It's the OCD}

This is the end of my article on...dragons? Oh yes! Buy my book.

And that's how you write a listicle.

SEO for Location

First of all: people are going to ask you to SEO[3] optimise their webpages a lot. Try not to let it[4] bother you. It doesn't bother me at all. Can you tell?

Anyway. To optimise a page for location is pretty simple. Advise your client to get on Google My Business and therefore on the Google Map. This boosts them immediately. You can even volunteer to do their listing.

Second, all of their webpages should mention where they are, at least once. Better yet, specific pages can be made up for each area they want to score higher in local listings for.

So if your client's business is in London, they may want a page for Slough, one for Watford, another for Dartford, and so on. What should each of these pages include? That's why I am here! It's one of my specialties because you can be as creative as the client allows.

The trick is to focus on the area and keep tying the area back to the product or service the client is trying to sell.

In this example I'll pretend I'm selling home improvement accessories in London. Every time I have italicised the words this represents a link to the destination I am talking about.

---

[3] Search Engine Optimisation
[4] It's called a Pleonasm. It's a redundant phase. Don't feel bad, I had to look it up. Other examples are ATM machine and PIN number. It makes my skin crawl.

Does Your Bracknell Home Need Updating? {H1 + Keywords}

If you happen to live in the Bracknell area, then the chances are your home isn't unique! In fact (random statistics always help everything) Bracknell is about to be home to 4,000 identical new houses, scheduled to be built by 2036. They might be new – but they will all be exactly, 100%, identical[5].

Who wants to live in a house that blends out with the crowd? If that doesn't sound like you, then **link to client's homepage** can help you!

Home Updates in Bracknell are Our Specialty! {H2}

We have everything you need to make your house pop. Sizzle, and stand out with a bang. I know I like to mix my idioms but don't hold it against my resting bitch face. Seriously – when did I start making grammar jokes??

Making Your Home Awesome {H2}

So how do you make your home as awesome as we can make it? Do these things.

Subheading in H3

Follow our instructions...

Subheading in H3

And you are sure to never fail!

---

[5] I would usually make this an endnote, but I don't want you to flip through to the last pages for a few words. In this endnote would be the source of this information. In this case; Homes & Property online; article "Buying in Bracknell", 15th April 2019.

Bracknell is at the Heart of *Our Brand* {H2}

Bracknell is where we were born and brought up. The icy waters of ***the Cut*** (Berkshire waterway) flow through many of our worker's veins. We have enjoyed sunny days in **Windsor Great Park**, spent afternoons enjoying the fresh air at **Lily Hill Park** – and have even taken the tour at Bagshot!

In our quest to bring product perfection to the residents of Bracknell, we have taken inspiration from the **Museum of Aviation**. In order to make our sleek, tailored, hand-crafted goods, we studied the ergonomic lines of the aged aircraft – just to bring familiarity, right to your door.

In Conclusion... {H2}

...You get the message. For 500 words tie in tourist attractions and local sights to the business, then round up with a conclusion. For a thousand words just keep going with H2s. In this case, I would use things like local sports teams for H3s.

Hopefully, that has covered all we need to know about making people's pages more location friendly. This is just one way, as well. I have also picked two or three features of a place and talked about them for 150 words each. Add on an intro and conclusion and you have an article.

Next, let's talk about writing web copy. Landing page writing is a little different in format. It is more focused on how it looks on the page and how it reads, as opposed to heading placement or structure.

Formatting Web Copy/Content

I left this till last because I genuinely hate it. If you do find me online to tell me how bad my grammar is, you will notice the difference in prices I charge. For blogging I charge the lower rate, for copy I stuck the price away up. I still do it once in a while... but dammit the client always wants to talk over the phone, and I have crippling social anxiety.

What do we mean by copy? Home pages, About Us pages, Product and Service Pages, Online Retail Descriptions, any little bit of writing between pictures on any given webpage.

The principle is the same as review writing – you are never, ever, negative. Find out what the brand persona is of the person you are writing for. Finding out how the founder came to be in this line of work is a good way to assign a story to a brand.

You do get to be a little creative, especially in the 'About Us' sections. You can talk passionately about whatever it is that the brand sells, make up stories about past happy customers, and generally speak with the voice of an expert. This is why I hate it. I'm not an expert. Before you start writing copy for a business you need to become that expert. It takes all day...

H1s and H2s don't really matter that much. What you will want is the address of the site they intend to use. There will be a blank template there (or there should be, if not, go back to the client for clarification) that will be filled with nonsensical words. 'Lorem Ipsum...' is usually how it starts.

It is your job to replace all the nonsense words with real ones. Worse, you need to go a step farther and make their product or service sound like the best money can buy. It's a little poetic in that you need to think about how it is going to be shaped when it is on the page.

I will do an example below. Let's pretend I am writing a home page for an art gallery in Cheshire.

ABC Arts, Cheshire. {H1}

Where life and art intertwine {Banners: there are always banners on a home page. These need a catchy title. The banner display may scroll through two or more catchy phrases, give them at least two}

Hello and welcome to our spectacular page full of stunning artwork. We display the highest quality pieces, contributed to our bespoke gallery space by local Cheshire artists.

{Image}

H3 – Free your Mind
Our gallery is free to browse.

H3 - Open 24/7
Our gallery is on call, 24 hours a day.

H3 – Affordable Artworks
Our masterpieces won't cost the Earth

H2 – Local Artwork, from Local Artists
If you live in Cheshire, then you might be familiar with the fabled works of our local artists. You may even know some of them! These special talents provide a variety of products for

your perusal. Delve into our sumptuous paintings and let yourself go!

Service Heading {H2}
Brief description of service

Exhibit Heading {H2}
Brief description of exhibit

You may wish to put the contact details of the firm at the bottom of the page. Only do this if they do not have a 'contact us' page planned. You should also link between the pages when you use phrases like 'contact us to find out more'.

And now you know that formatting web pages isn't as hard as it looks. Except for the whole 'making yourself an expert in a few hours' thing, you are good to go. This is one of the many reasons they tell you to write about what you know…

Other Online Writing Formats

There are lots of different types of article, but I have tried to cover most, below.

Writing 'How-to' Guides

The format for a guide is exactly the same as it is with an article. Make sure that each step is clearly outlined. It might help you to write your headings out beforehand. For example: "a five step guide to starting a fire in the wilderness" would involve one H1 title, two H2s, maybe three. Lastly, the five steps as H3s, followed by an H2 conclusion.

The longer the guide is, the more points you use. Similarly to a listicle, between 7 and 10 points per thousand words is enough. 3-5 points per five hundred words is a good way to calculate space.

Writing Product Descriptions

If you have the product then fantastic; describe it.

You will not have the product. You will, in fact, be sitting at home behind your laptop. Don't sweat it. Other people have bought the product, used it, and left reviews all over the internet. Piece together what it does from a combination of these and the manufacturer's description.

Make it sound like the best thing ever to have been invented. Always be positive unless otherwise instructed by the client.

Writing Reviews

You shouldn't really do this unless you have personally tried the product. That being said, the process is similar to product descriptions. Other people have already reviewed them. Just to be clear, I'm not saying you plagiarise; I'm saying to take the idea, not the words.

So if a reviewer says their new hair dryer is awesome for big curls, you can catch that idea and turn it into something else. I might say that the dryer has "obviously been designed for ladies with larger-than-life hairdo's". I might say that it "gives fantastic volume" since it is good for bounce...

I hope you are with me. Never steal work, even if it is from a backstreet blog you don't think anyone will ever read. A quick internet search and your reputation will be obliterated.

Writing eBooks

I am against this as a rule. It's advice going around about how to make a passive income – and each article tells them to make an eBook. So they make one, using you, and you never see any royalties.

My issue is part – well I could write that myself and keep the royalties, and part – not everyone has got a book in them. You're a writer, or you're not a writer.

On the other hand (and to be an absolute hypocrite) I work with a client who is making a series of kid's books. I made an exception because she was desperate and because I have never written for children before. It's working out well. However, in future I will ask for royalties plus a fee. Get myself some of that passive income...

Tell the client to give you a detailed account of what happens in each chapter. Work on a chapter at a time, have them pay you at the end of each one. I have known clients to drop off the face of the Earth. Usually after they realise the costs of an eBook mean they will need to sell at least a hundred to make a profit.

Format is easy. Chapter heading is H1, everything else is H2 or H3. Go where the client leads you. Give it your best but save your style and identifiable phrases to yourself. It's their book, not yours. Another reason why you probably shouldn't do it.

Editing

Hell yes. Bring it on. Edit anything and everything. Once you have stumbled through enough articles you get a feel for it. The whole reason I am sitting here at 23:17 at night on a Wednesday writing this dang thing is because I edit.

I have been given so many articles written by folk that didn't know how to write articles; that it hurts my head to think about. I am a great believer in getting things right the first-time round. I freely admit that I make mistakes just like the next person. However, if my main contribution on this Earth is to prevent others having to repeat themselves; then I will die happy.

News Reports

Eeewwww. I hate these but only because I suck at them. As you can tell from this whole book, I am not big on writing 'dry'. I don't know if that's what other people call it but it's my term for that bland, boring, reporting of facts that makes newsreaders sound like robots. That's the tone to shoot for.

A pro tip for getting past plagiarism checks is to paraphrase the quotes. I know that it's the same reason the truth gets lost in the wafts of media rewrites – but it is the best way to convince the plagiarism software that you aren't stealing work. In every news report the quotes are often the same. It can hit you anywhere between 1 and 5% if you're not careful.

As a rule of thumb news reports don't care much for headings. 1 x H1 centred in bold, a by line or a subtitle, and away you go. I'd add another H2 in there because I wouldn't be able to help myself – but the editor would most likely cut it out.

Press Releases

Another thing I hate writing (I swear, give me an endless sea of five hundred word blogs and I'd happily make my millions) are press releases. The announcement of a new product, or product line, or the announcement of their AGM/convention/a new market they have accessed.

This kind of writing is full of attention grabbing headlines. Of course, it's not really about the H1 and H2, it's about what the sub-headers say. Witty, eye catching, lots of alliteration, make things rhyme, use a literary device of some kind. A press release is like a news report but with the ability to make you stop what you are doing and pay attention. Kind of like a news report by John Snow[6].

More Information

There are a hundred other little bits and pieces, but these pages contain the brunt of it all. No doubt as soon as I send this to print, everything I have missed will come back to me. There's a chance I will do another book in the future but in the meantime, you can catch me at my blog: KatrionaWrites on Blogger and other Social Media outlets near you.

---

[6] That's the clever C4 guy, not the one that doesn't know anything.

Following the Brief

This is something that you really need to pay attention to. The farther you are from the brief, the farther you are from the client's needs. If you aren't giving them what they asked for then you need to go back and forth until they're happy – and that wastes everyone's time.

Make no mistake: a single typo and the article will be sent back to you. It does not matter to 90% of clients that they could save a week of time if they saved the document and fixed it themselves: they will send it back to you. They will. You won't get paid until they release the funds... you get the idea.

Following a brief is akin to when the teacher spent a year in Higher English trying to teach you how to deconstruct essay questions. Pay attention. Give them exactly what they ask for. Sometimes, if you have to, sarcastically... but always what they ask for.

There are very few times that you can get away with working outside the brief – but you really ought to clear it with the client beforehand. More often than not, if you disagree with the content then you won't reach an agreement with the client. Once in a great while you can write exactly what the client wants and savagely cut them with their own words...

I'll only give one example. A woman who sold essential oils didn't want me to mention some of the cancer-causing side effects of a certain type of oil she sold. I disagreed. In the end I refused to write for her. She presumably found another writer.

Follow the brief. That is the lesson here. It will save you back and forth time with the client. If you don't know something, ask them. Otherwise you will produce work no one wants.

The way I work is to read the brief, write the thing, then read the brief again before I hand it back. That way you always answer every point. On the other hand I have also been issued a title by a client, only to have it given back to me with a note that they didn't like the title... Some days you just can't win.

What Not To Do

As an online content writer there are things that you shouldn't do. That is to say: You can do them if you want to, but you probably won't be doing yourself any favours. I'll list as many as I can below.

1 – Agreeing to Post to Client's Sites

Take an example... A client approached me and asked for a few blogs posts a month. I said that's easy enough, sent him some blog suggestions and he sent me back a list of the ones he was OK with. My first mistake was sending the list for free. My second mistake was trying to impress the client by making my blog titles really difficult... I then had to write some really difficult blog posts.

Lastly, he asked me to post them to his website. Stupidly I agreed. I thought it'd be a click and drag site. It was a stupendously complex WordPress the likes of which would confuse Bill Gates. I gave up after two hours of wasted time and confessed I couldn't do it. You know what that client did? He said, "OK then, just write them."

I got the same frigging money for doing it without posting them. I saved myself at least twenty hours. Most of the time the client will spend hours and hours managing their site or will outsource it to someone else. The posting of things to that site should not be the responsibility of an online content writer you just met over the internet. Genuinely, some people are grossly misled.

By all means do it – but make sure you charge as an extra service. It's a special skill, not one all clients should expect for free.

It's like asking a plumber to fix the electric. I can't even...

2 – Be A Social Media Manager

My goodness me. I turn down a request to be someone's voice on social media on a weekly basis. Can you write the content for my x site? Great! Can you log in as me and post it? No? Why not? Aren't you a writer?

At that point the fourth law of diction allows you to knock them out with a thesaurus.

Same as before: you are not a social media poster, manager, or stand-in. They can post their own crap. You only need to write it for them. Nine times out of ten this customer actually wants to hire a Social Media Management Firm but can't afford it.

Again, do it for them just make sure you charge them through the teeth for it. It is a special service, an optional extra, and a skill not everyone has.

3 – Write their (School) Essay

I have had so very many non-English speakers approach me and ask me in broken words if I can write their School/College/University/English lesson paper for them. No, no, no. So much "no". It's wrong on too many levels. You make a fast buck but there is a strong chance they will get caught for cheating. Teachers aren't stupid. If he or she doesn't know what 'exam' means they aren't going to be using eight syllable words in their paper – which, as a writer, you can't help.

4 – Write "Something About xxx"

They come to you with a broad topic – say social media, for example – and then ask you to "write something about it." So you go away and write about social media marketing in 2020. They come back and say no, they are an influencer, their clients don't care about that. Their followers want to know how they can set up a twitter account... duh!

Again... Thesaurus... one quick swipe...

This wastes your time, wastes their time, and generally has you doing things fourteen times. Tell them to sort out a topic heading and don't write for them when they come back again. Which they will. There is a high chance you are the only writer who will put up with their *hit.

5 – Give Yourself Ridiculous Deadlines
Some of us have a 3k daily word count, some of us have 500 words. That's fine. Manage this as you see fit. Don't be overloading yourself with too many promises, twenty clients, and a full calendar. Work however much you can fit in comfortably around your day. The only other option is to burn out.

Now let's face it. The majority of us are doing this as a day job and writing our fiction at night. If you fall into this boat, then you are at high risk of burning out. You hit your daily wordcount, close your pc and leave it till the morning. It's hard to keep that motivation.

At the end of the day, it is the same as any other job. If you had the energy to come home from the Supermarket and write, then I have every confidence that you can find enough energy to write after spending a day on Fiverr, People Per Hour, iWriter, or Upwork. I have faith in you. Just know your limits.

6 – 'Forget' links, references, or citations
In my opinion (which we all know isn't that humble), the link is replacing the citation. The internet was literally invented to store the entirety of human knowledge. If you can't find the experiment, study, theory, or quote online then it probably didn't happen. Why bother citing the book, page number, author, and year of publication – when you could just highlight the section and link directly to the data. If anyone cares enough, they will follow it.

What you don't do – and this very day I had to fix something of this nature – is forgo links completely. If you don't link, you need to put references at the bottom of the article. I add them as endnotes for every point that I need to argue. Any info you use that isn't linked, or referenced, might as well be made up.

This is the internet and people like facts. Check your facts, link to your facts, nobody can argue with you. Added bonus: once you get good at this there isn't a single social media troll in the world able to stand against you. Once you get to mastery levels your fingertips will move faster than your mind does.

I am adding a later amendment to the above. This week I had a client who didn't agree with the historical article I wrote. I cited and linked to maybe 10 sources? The client's version didn't match my sources version, so he didn't like the article.

I didn't argue. I just told him I wasn't the writer he needed and gave him a refund.

7 – Plagiarise

When you are a writer and you plagiarise, something amazing happens. All of the other writers in your city crawl out from under their desks to beat you with their unfinished manuscripts. It's called death by a thousand (paper) cuts. I genuinely don't know if I just stole that joke… please don't kill me.

Don't steal someone else's words. It's not cool. It's easier to write your own and you don't risk your reputation. Which leads us to the next rule…

8 – Check you haven't plagiarised

Sometimes you do it accidentally. You pick up something subconsciously, think it's a great idea, and file it away for later. I mentioned plagiarism software before and there are both free and paid programs out there. Check everything before you hand it in. As a bonus tip – fictional writers always need to be checking their book titles before it gets to publication.

9 – Website Designing

Just say no folks. It's like a bad disease. One client asks and before you know it, they all want it.

You're a writer. If you need to spend three hours negotiating their website, you are wasting valuable writing time. Plus you're not a web designer. Sack that. On the other hand – if you are good at it, do it and charge extra.

10 – Spend Hours Hunting Images Down

You an spend days finding the perfect image for a client; or you could just tell them that you are a writer and not spend days at it. The choice is yours. Every hour you spend photo hunting is an hour you could have written a thousand words.

This is just a guideline, remember. Personally I arrange my time so that I charge more for web copy. If you happen to be better at listicles and rubbish at blogs, price accordingly. Your cheapest product should be whatever you can do the fastest.

Clients... Where to Find them and What to do with them Once you Have Them?

Clients are the heart of any business. You need them to operate but sometimes you would rather put them in the bin instead of the work. It happens. You can't get on with everyone you meet in your life.

Where do you find new clients? Everywhere. Let's discuss.

Finding New Clients

I constantly come across new writers who are complaining about how much they can sell an article for, so let's be clear about this. How much you genuinely want to work as a writer will affect how much you are willing to sacrifice. You need experience more than anything else. If you have to sacrifice by doing two or three articles for a pittance to get that experience, then I say do it. I would rather be a working writer who swallowed their pride a little, than someone who calls themselves a writer but has never been paid.

The hard part is knowing when to re-price and how high to push it. As your ability grows your price should grow... but take it with a little humble pie. Far too many writers – usually ones that are too busy correcting people's grammar on t'internet to actually write anything – complain there's no work. There's plenty of work. If nobody wants to buy your first article for fifty bucks that's perfectly understandable.

I'm not saying don't aim high: I'm saying you don't walk into a business you have no knowledge of and immediately start moaning that nobody recognises your talent. Go out and show them how talented you are. You have to, if you want to be able to show them what you can do. If this industry is meant for you and you write every day anyway - being paid for it is just a bonus.

So on that note...

You can write to a website owner and say "hey, your website isn't great, I can re-write it for you for $50". Or you can write to a website owner and ask to re-write their website for $50 and include some previous work. I know who gets the work in that scenario. Start small if you have to. Every opening is a way in, no matter how insignificant.

Approaching Unsolicited

This works if you are a friendly sort who can pick holes in something without being condescending. When you approach website owners like this, they probably wrote their content themselves and, let's be frank, most of them will have bruised egos if you tell them their pages read terribly. Be gentle.

Start locally, would be my advice. Email local businesses and with examples of blogs or home pages and just let them know you exist. The chances are they will ask you to do a test blog just because you live in their area. Work your way up from there.

Do not – and I mean this unconditionally – approach other writers and ask them for work. They are in your position. It's insulting because it implies that they outsource and don't write things themselves. One of the worst kept secrets in the industry is that most 'posters' on company blogs don't actually exist. They are us, disguised as a single character.

You can approach big businesses, but they are likely to have staff writers. A good idea if looking for work in this way is to keep your own blog on a variety of subjects. You can then send them relevant work, should you have it to hand. If you want to become a staff writer for a big business, then get on job sites. If you are in the UK, Indeed always has some good ones. Usually they are based in London. We Scots have to work remotely.

Using Sites

I am a big fan of the work site. I know a whole bunch of artists who refuse to use them because they think they take advantage of the worker. I think that taking advantage of an artist is paying them in exposure. I also think it is my own responsibility to set a standard and price that entices the buyer. Generally speaking, if the price is too low a good client won't just tell you – they'll tip you. They'll even encourage you to charge more.

OK, so 90% of people aren't that nice but the ten percent are the ones you want to work with. I am a big advocator of using the sites as a form of protection for both parties, too. If you go through (for example) People Per Hour, you are ensured a payment as much as the buyer is ensured a finished product. Sure they take a huge cut, but you are paying for a protection.

Do what everyone else does, factor the commission into your costs and work with the client long enough that the rate falls. I would advise that you only use a site from your own country though, simply because of the rate of exchange. You are already losing a commission, don't compound the problem.

Other suggested sites include Upwork, iWriter, which I have been told to try but haven't yet, and Fiverr. Fiverr is very competitively priced. I find PPH easier to work with. Of course, it is entirely up to you.

Free-for-All Clients

I often work with clients over email that have been attracted to my brand over time. If you are going to go pro with this, get a blog, logo, and distinct style of your own. If you post enough of it all over the internet, people will start following you. Eventually some of them will message you for business.

You will not believe how many people you know that are in the website business. Once you declare that you write for sites, they will either flock to you or refuse to believe you. It is your job to prove them wrong.

Dealing with Bad Clients

I have a rubbish BS detector. Absolutely awful. I'm just about as gullible as they come. I think it is a sign of honesty that I believe what people tell me. However, in a business environment this led to me repeating the same lesson many times over.

If it looks like a skunk, acts like a skunk, and moves like a skunk – you don't need to wait to be sprayed with butt juice to know it's a skunk.

When a client approaches you with an attitude, demands you do what they say (immediately) and tries to negotiate a lesser rate; do yourself a favour and just say no from the start. They are trouble. Here's the most important thing to remember:

You don't owe anyone a damned thing.

You got out of the rat race and started doing this for yourself, for a reason. If the client is an asshat, there is no need for you to keep battering your head against that particular wall. Say no, move on, get the next client.

A Few Final Thoughts

This is where I sum it all up by telling you it was all just a dream and that's why there are so many plot-holes. However, since this is nonfiction, I will bid you good luck, instead.

One thing I would caution you about is a warning against becoming one of the literati. These are people who condescend with grammar, who patronise with pronunciations and who are the reason why some people are instantly put off literature. Just don't do it. Don't hover, waiting on your friends to make a mistake. They will stop inviting you to parties.

The literary world is evolving. It's difficult to find a foothold as a writer who gets paid for their work. Whether you write first class fiction or whether you are writing scripts for porn movies – it doesn't matter. To leave you with the inspirational words of (everyone's hero) Stephen King:

> "If you wrote something for which someone paid you a check, if you cashed the check and it didn't bounce, and if you then paid the light bill with the money, **I consider you talented.**"

Online content is in such high demand right now that you need to be genuinely terrible at your job to not find work (If this is you then I'm sorry; this book probably can't help you). Don't be sad about it. Either go back to fiction or tell me to do one. It's your dream, not mine. Either way: you don't need to put up with anyone's attitude, judgement, or hypocrisy... Including mine. You do you.

If that was the only lesson you learned today, I will be happy with that.

Printed in Great Britain
by Amazon